Original title:
Wonders of the Wind

Copyright © 2024 Creative Arts Management OÜ
All rights reserved.

Author: Hugo Fitzgerald
ISBN HARDBACK: 978-9916-90-114-4
ISBN PAPERBACK: 978-9916-90-115-1

Crystal Clear Thoughts

In the stillness of the night,
Whispers dance in candlelight.
Thoughts like ripples on a stream,
Fleeting shadows of a dream.

Words unspoken fill the air,
Thoughts unravel, thread and bare.
Truths emerge, so bright, divine,
Crystal clear, as stars align.

Moments grasped with gentle hands,
In the quiet, wisdom stands.
Echoes soft of days gone by,
Painting visions in the sky.

In this space, the heart finds peace,
From tangled webs, a sweet release.
With each breath, a promise sworn,
In crystal clarity, reborn.

The Flow of Quiet Moments

Time drifts softly, like a stream,
In the hush of twilight's dream.
Gentle breezes call my name,
Filling silence, like a flame.

Colors fade as day turns shy,
Whispers cradle, soft and spry.
In the stillness, thoughts collide,
In this haven, we abide.

Moments linger, stretched and thin,
Where the world's chaos grows dim.
Here we wander, lose our way,
In the quiet, night and day.

In the flow, a heartbeat slows,
Embracing all that silence knows.
Captured softly, time moves on,
In this stillness, we belong.

Tails of the Celestial Wanderer

In the night, a star takes flight,
Trailing tales of ancient light.
Whispers of the cosmic roam,
Guiding hearts far from home.

Comets dance in radiant sweep,
Through the dark, their secrets keep.
Galaxies spin, a timeless show,
Eternity's song, soft and slow.

Flickers of Windborne Light

Across the fields, the breezes stray,
Carrying whispers of the day.
Sunlight dapples on the grass,
Moments fleeting, as they pass.

In the trees, the shadows play,
Flickers bright that chase the gray.
Nature's brush paints scenes divine,
In every gust, a perfect line.

Laughter of the Open Sky

Above the clouds, the laughter rolls,
Echoes of unburdened souls.
Joyful winds that twist and spin,
Celebrating where we've been.

With every gust, a story shared,
In the vastness, nobody cared.
The sky unfolds, a canvas wide,
Where dreams and hopes can freely glide.

Tales Written on the Breath of the Earth

Beneath the soil, the whispers grow,
Stories deep where rivers flow.
Mountains stand, guardians old,
Tales of magic yet untold.

In the air, the echoes sing,
Of life that blooms in every spring.
Nature's voice, pure and true,
Crafting legends, fresh as dew.

Haikus on the Horizon

Waves kiss the soft sand,
Whispers of the sea breeze,
Footprints left behind,
Sunrise paints the calm sky.

Clouds drift in stillness,
Birds dance in morning light,
Nature's gentle hum,
Awakens dreams anew.

Veils of the Sky

Twilight drapes the world,
Stars flicker into view,
Moonlight spills like silk,
Night's whispers fill the air.

Veils of mist arise,
Softly cloaking the earth,
Hidden secrets bloom,
In shadows' gentle grasp.

Celestial Drafts

Comets streak the night,
Galaxies swirl above,
Infinite wonders,
Dancing in the vast dark.

Shooting stars ignite,
Dreams cast on cosmic winds,
Hope in every spark,
Stories of worlds unseen.

Songs of the Swaying Grasses

Whispers of the fields,
Grasses sway in the breeze,
Nature's soft chorus,
Echoes of summer's song.

Golden hues collide,
Dance under the bright sun,
Life in every blade,
Harmony's sweet embrace.

Fluttering Feathers

In the breeze, they softly sway,
Dancing light, they steal away.
Whispers of the skies above,
Carrying the songs of love.

Every color, a tale to tell,
From gardens rich where they do dwell.
In the sunlight, shadows play,
Fluttering, they steal the day.

Wings that brush against the sun,
A gentle flight has just begun.
Through the air, they weave and glide,
On hidden winds, they take their ride.

With each flutter, a dream takes flight,
In the fading glow of light.
Echoes linger, soft and bright,
As day turns gently into night.

Carried Dreams on Currents

On silver streams of azure skies,
My dreams like birds begin to rise.
With every gust, they swirl and spin,
A journey new, where hope begins.

Floating softly, free and bold,
Whispers of the tales I've told.
In currents swift, they find their way,
To lands where night turns into day.

Gentle breezes guide them far,
Like wishes cast upon a star.
With every sigh, they drift and weave,
In the fabric of what I believe.

On waves of air, so sweetly light,
They sail through dreams, with pure delight.
Each thought a feather, soft and warm,
Riding high, away from harm.

Nature's Breath

In every rustle, every sigh,
Nature speaks, the world nearby.
Fragrant blooms and whispered trees,
Together dancing in the breeze.

Through mountain peaks and valleys wide,
In every tide, the earth's great stride.
Each heartbeat echoes in the glade,
As life unfolds, our fears do fade.

From morning light to twilight's fade,
In every shadow, love is laid.
The gentle streams and rivers run,
A melody beneath the sun.

In hollow caves or open skies,
Every beauty beneath our eyes.
Breath of life in colors blend,
Nature's dance, forever penned.

The Invisible Touch

A gentle hand, so soft, so kind,
In moments shared, our hearts entwined.
The warmth of love, a silent thread,
Binding us where words have fled.

In tender glances, secrets bloom,
A soft embrace, dispelling gloom.
Each fleeting touch, a spark ignites,
In hushed whispers, love ignites.

Across the room, a gaze can say,
More than words can every day.
The spaces filled with what we feel,
An unseen bond that's pure and real.

Though invisible, it's always there,
A silent promise, sweet and rare.
In every heartbeat, every sigh,
The invisible touch, you and I.

Lullabies of the Air

Whispers dance on twilight's breeze,
Soft the tones that put hearts at ease.
Crickets hum their velvet song,
In the night where dreams belong.

Stars above with gentle light,
Guide the weary through the night.
Each lullaby, a tender thread,
Woven softly in my head.

Veils of the Airborne Spirits

On wings of grace, they drift and play,
Veils of mist in soft array.
Dancing shadows, soft and bright,
Spirits whisper through the night.

They carry tales of love and loss,
In every breeze, the winds emboss.
Veils that shimmer, drift away,
Hiding secrets in their sway.

Echoes of the Wandering Zephyr

The zephyr calls with a curious sigh,
Echoes linger as it glides by.
Through the trees, it weaves a tune,
A melody beneath the moon.

Whispers float on currents sweet,
Footsteps of time in rhythmic beat.
In every echo, life is spun,
The wandering zephyr, ever fun.

The Mysterious Breath of Nature

In silence deep, a breath is caught,
Nature's pulse in every thought.
Leaves converse with the gentle air,
Secrets shared, both rich and rare.

Mountains stand with ancient grace,
Holding whispers of time and space.
A breath of life, so strong and pure,
In nature's heart, we find our cure.

Sighs from the Horizon

Soft whispers float on evening air,
Golden rays fade beyond despair.
Clouds cradle secrets of the past,
Promises linger, fading fast.

Waves caress the sandy shore,
Echoing dreams we can't ignore.
Time dances lightly in the dusk,
While shadows murmur, dawn's a must.

The breeze carries tales untold,
Of wanderers brave and bold.
With every sigh, a story breathes,
In the heart, the spirit weaves.

As night descends, stars will gleam,
Illuminating every dream.
Horizon beckons, always near,
In its grasp, we shed the fear.

Songs of the Wandering Tempest

Whirling winds in a cosmic dance,
Nature sings in wild romance.
Lightning strikes the silent night,
Awakening souls with its light.

Storm clouds gather, shadows loom,
Thunder's pulse brings forth the gloom.
Yet in chaos, beauty thrives,
A raw reminder that love survives.

Raindrops join in symphonic play,
Harmonizing with the skies' gray.
Each gust carries a heartfelt cry,
A lullaby from way up high.

Tempest twirls, breaking the calm,
Spreading ferocity like a balm.
As it travels, profound and free,
Songs of the tempest set us free.

In the Embrace of Cyclones

Whirling forces twist and bend,
Nature's wrath, an unseen friend.
Caught within the cyclone's hold,
Moments of courage, fierce and bold.

In swirling winds, we find our way,
Guided by hope, come what may.
Chaos reigns, yet still we soar,
In the heart of the storm, we implore.

Eyes wide open, heartbeats race,
In the eye, we find our place.
A fleeting calm amid the strife,
Cyclones remind us of life's life.

Battered but strong, we rise anew,
Learning from the winds that blew.
In every tempest, there's a chance,
To find our voice, to take a stance.

A Canvas Painted by the Breeze

Upon the canvas, colors swirl,
Gentle strokes as dreams unfurl.
Breezes whisper secrets low,
Painting visions, letting go.

Emerald fields and azure skies,
Nature's palette, everwise.
With every gust, horizons shift,
Artistry in each gentle lift.

Blossoms dance in sunlight's grin,
With each breeze, a tale begins.
A tapestry woven from the air,
Life's delicate brushstrokes, rare.

As twilight fades, the colors blend,
A masterpiece that knows no end.
In the silence, beauty stays,
A canvas painted by the breeze.

The Sky's Gentle Caress

In the morning light so soft,
The clouds drift by, like thoughts aloft.
Whispers of warmth touch the ground,
A secret embrace, peace found.

With colors blush, the sun ascends,
Beneath its glow, the day transcends.
A gentle breeze plays in the trees,
Nature's sigh, a sweet release.

As twilight deepens, shadows grow,
The stars peek out, a gentle show.
In this calm, the heart can rest,
The sky above, a tranquil nest.

Night wraps the world in velvet grace,
Yet still, the dreams take flight in space.
With every glance, the heart learns fast,
The sky's caress, forever vast.

Tapestry of Fluttering Leaves

Colors dance upon the trees,
Golden hues in the soft breeze.
Each rustle tells a tale anew,
Of changing seasons, life's debut.

Crisp air whispers through the boughs,
Nature sings, and the woodland bows.
Leaves celebrate their final flight,
Painting the ground in soft twilight.

Amidst the oaks, a symphony,
Of swaying branches, wild and free.
Every flutter, a gentle sigh,
In this tapestry, dreams can fly.

A carpet made of colors bright,
Inviting all to share the light.
In this embrace, old stories weave,
A dance of time, we can believe.

Voices Through the Canopy

In the depths of the greenest wood,
Whispers echo, understood.
The branches hold the tales of old,
Of spirits, dreams, and truths untold.

Birds converse in melodies,
Filling the air with harmonies.
A rustling sound, a fleeting deer,
Nature's voice, so pure and clear.

In the hush, a secret shared,
A bond with earth, truly cared.
Through the leaves, the stories flow,
Guiding hearts where kindness grows.

As daylight fades and shadows creep,
The forest hums, lulling to sleep.
Voices linger, soft and low,
Through the canopy, love will grow.

A Symphony of Blustering Air

In the mountains, winds collide,
With wild abandon, they swiftly glide.
A symphony of nature's might,
In every gust, a pure delight.

Through valleys deep and fields so wide,
The gusts of change no one can hide.
They sing of storms, and sunlit days,
In every note, the heart conveys.

Leaves are tossed in playful dance,
Under the spell of wind's romance.
A whisper here, a howl up there,
In noisy echo, life lays bare.

As twilight falls, the breezes sigh,
A lullaby beneath the sky.
In harmony with earth, we stand,
A symphony by nature's hand.

Ribbons of Memory

In the attic of dreams, they weave,
Soft threads of time, we believe.
Faded whispers on fragile lace,
Stories linger in their embrace.

Colors of laughter, shades of tears,
Bound by the fabric of forgotten years.
Each ribbon tells a tale, it's true,
A tapestry of me and you.

In corners dark, they softly gleam,
Echoing pasts that drift like a dream.
Through storms of change, they find their way,
Guiding hearts to a brighter day.

In silence, they dance, forever bright,
Illuminating shadows with their light.
Ribbons of memory, strong and thin,
Holding the moments where we begin.

Free as a Breeze

I feel the wind upon my face,
A gentle caress, a soft embrace.
It whispers secrets through the trees,
Dancing lightly, free as a breeze.

Clouds drift lazily in the sky,
Painting tales as they float by.
With every gust, the world can sing,
Nature's joy in a vibrant spring.

Through fields of gold, the wildflowers sway,
Chasing the sun through the brightening day.
The laughter of children, pure and unchecked,
Boundless as the love we elect.

With open hearts, we learn to fly,
On wings of dreams, we'll touch the sky.
No chains can hold what longs to roam,
In the embrace of the earth, we'll find our home.

Whispers from the Unknown

In the depth of night, a voice arrives,
Secrets woven in shadowed sighs.
Echoes linger, soft and low,
Whispers beckon from below.

They speak of worlds we cannot see,
Of ancient paths and lost decree.
In silence deep, their stories flow,
Carrying dreams of long ago.

With every glance, the air turns thick,
Mysteries spiral, time's clock ticks.
Curiosity, a wild fire,
Awakening souls to deep desire.

The unknown calls, a siren's song,
Inviting hearts to come along.
In the dance of fate, we boldly stand,
Hand in hand with the unseen hand.

Flying Thoughts

Like birds that soar, so thoughts take flight,
Gliding on wings of day and night.
Chasing dreams through skies so wide,
In every heart, they seek to hide.

Whispers of hope, they flutter near,
In laughter's echo, they disappear.
Caught in a maze, in webs of mind,
Fleeting moments, hard to find.

They pirouette on the breeze of chance,
Lost in the rhythm, a timeless dance.
Through valleys deep, and mountains tall,
We find our way, we hear their call.

In the stillness, they whisper clear,
Reminding us of all we hold dear.
Flying thoughts, both wild and free,
Trace the paths of our memory.

Whispers in the Breeze

Gentle whispers dance on leaves,
A story told by rustling trees.
Softly weaving tales of old,
In nature's arms, a truth unfolds.

Sunlight glimmers through the branches,
Casting shadows in soft prances.
Each breeze a note, a fleeting sigh,
Echoes of the earth's soft cry.

Beneath the sky, their secrets twine,
In vibrant hues, the world aligns.
Moments linger in the air,
As whispers linger everywhere.

In the silence, hearts can hear,
The softest breath, the pulse so near.
Nature's voice, a tender blend,
In whispers, all our fears can mend.

Dances of Invisible Currents

In the twilight, shadows sway,
Invisible currents find their play.
With every gust, memories tease,
A dance of life upon the breeze.

Whirls of joy and hints of sorrow,
Each movement holds a bright tomorrow.
Fluttering dreams take flight anew,
In currents where the heart beats true.

A gentle touch, unseen embrace,
The dance unfolds in sacred space.
Like spirits moving, swift and free,
A timeless waltz for you and me.

With every swirl, our lives conjoin,
In whispered rhythms, hearts align.
In these currents, let us flow,
Together where the wild winds blow.

The Sky's Gentle Serenade

Above the world, the sky sings low,
A gentle serenade in the glow.
Clouds drift softly, dreams take flight,
As stars awaken in the night.

Moonbeams dance on silver streams,
Reflecting all our hidden dreams.
With every note, the cosmos glows,
A symphony that ebbs and flows.

The sun will rise, painting the dawn,
With melodies of life reborn.
In harmony, the earth will sway,
To nature's song, a bright ballet.

So listen close, for in the air,
A gentle serenade flows there.
With every breath, the world we'll greet,
In this sweet lullaby, so sweet.

Secrets Carried by the Gales

The gales at dusk, they softly speak,
With tales of wonder, bold and meek.
Carrying whispers from afar,
Each secret held beneath the stars.

Through valleys deep and mountains high,
The winds will carry, never shy.
They weave the stories of the night,
In breezy paths, they take their flight.

With every gust, a truth revealed,\nThe heart of nature, gently healed.
Listen close, for in the air,
Are secrets, tender and rare.

In swirling winds, our hopes reside,
Like fragile dreams on nature's tide.
Embrace the gales, let them unfold,
The secrets of the winds retold.

Laughing Clouds

Fluffy white in the sky,
They dance and sway with glee,
Whispers of joy float by,
Floating wild and free.

They gather, twist, and shout,
Rainbows arch from their sides,
No reason for a pout,
With them, love abides.

Filling hearts with delight,
Painting shadows with light,
In their playful embrace,
Life finds a joyous space.

As they drift overhead,
They weave dreams in the blue,
With laughter, they spread
A comfort pure and true.

Gentle Breaths of Tomorrow

Morning breaks with soft grace,
Whispers of hope arise,
Birds in flight, a sweet chase,
Under open skies.

Each breath brings a new start,
Awakening the day,
Nature plays its sweet part,
In its wondrous display.

Dreams unfurl like the leaves,
In sunlight's warm embrace,
A promise that it believes
In the future's face.

With every gentle sigh,
The world begins to bloom,
With love's tender lullaby,
Chasing away the gloom.

Portals to Possibility

Open doors in the mind,
Where dreams can freely soar,
Imagination unconfined,
Inviting you to explore.

Colors swirl and collide,
Worlds crafted with pure light,
With each vibrant stride,
New paths come into sight.

Echoes of laughter ring,
As thoughts begin to flow,
Each notion takes to wing,
In realms only we know.

With every step we take,
New destinies unfold,
In the magic we make,
Our stories will be told.

Essence of the Atmosphere

Breezes play through the trees,
A gentle, soothing touch,
Whispers carried with ease,
Nature's heart beats as such.

Each raindrop, a soft kiss,
A promise from the sky,
All that we dare to miss,
In every breath we sigh.

Stars twinkle in the night,
A canvas deep and vast,
Guiding souls with their light,
Echoes of the past.

In the stillness, we find,
The pulse of life so near,
In the essence entwined,
A world we hold so dear.

Flight of the Feathered Thoughts

A whisper of wings takes to the sky,
Carried by dreams that wander high.
Each flutter a story lost in the breeze,
Drifting like thoughts that yearn to be free.

In currents unseen, they dance and glide,
Painting the air where hopes reside.
With colors of joy, they paint the dawn,
These feathered thoughts that travel on.

From tree to tree, their journeys unfold,
In the sacred silence, secrets told.
They echo the laughter of skies above,
In the flight of a heart, filled with love.

So let them soar, let them explore,
Each delicate whisper, an open door.
For in their flight, we too can see,
The beauty of thoughts, wild and free.

Mists and Migrations

Veils of gray drape the quiet land,
Whispers of secrets, soft as sand.
Foggy tendrils weave through the trees,
Carrying tales on the cool, crisp breeze.

Birds gather, a chorus of song,
As nature guides them, where they belong.
Through mists that cloak the early morn,
New journeys arise, new paths are born.

The world transforms in this hazy light,
Where shadows blend with morning bright.
Each step a promise, each beat a vow,
In the dance of life, we find our how.

So let the mists embrace our fears,
And carry away our silent tears.
For migrations teach us, through silent rhyme,
The beauty of change, the gift of time.

Celestial Currents Unseen

Stars whisper softly in the night sky,
With strokes of light that seem to fly.
Guided by forces we cannot grasp,
They dance in patterns, in cosmic clasp.

Planets curve in a graceful arc,
Traveling paths igniting the dark.
In silence, they spin, a celestial show,
Spreading the seeds of what we may know.

These currents unseen, a heavenly tide,
Pulling our hearts where mysteries hide.
In the vastness above, we search for signs,
Connecting our souls through invisible lines.

So look to the stars, let your spirit rise,
In the twilight hours, embrace the skies.
For in this vast cosmos, we find our way,
In the currents of night, come what may.

The Playful Touch of a Gale

The wind whips playfully through the trees,
Caressing the leaves with gentle ease.
A laugh in the air, a brightening cheer,
The playful touch of a gale draws near.

It spins through meadows, a joyous flight,
Whirling the petals, a beautiful sight.
Every gust brings a story anew,
In the dance of the elements, freedom rings true.

Clouds tumble and roll, a soft ballet,
As the breeze invites them to join the play.
Through fields and valleys, the whispers call,
In nature's embrace, we find our all.

So let the gale tickle your soul,
With laughter and light, it makes us whole.
For in its wildness, we find our grace,
The playful touch of a gale we embrace.

Dance of the Gale

In whispers soft, the breeze calls out,
With twirls and spins, it swirls about.
Leaves flutter down, a soft ballet,
In nature's arms, they sway and play.

Clouds drift by, the sun peeks through,
The dance of the gale, a vibrant hue.
Each moment shines, a fleeting glance,
In the embrace of the wind's sweet dance.

Mountains echo the song of the day,
With every gust, the trees sway.
The world alive, in rhythm's sway,
Together we move, come what may.

The sky a canvas, painted bright,
As day turns to dusk, and fades from sight.
In the closing dance, the stars appear,
With the gale beside, there's nothing to fear.

Secrets Carried on Air

In gentle breath, the secrets glide,
Stories whispered, the wind can't hide.
Carried forth on currents fine,
Like tender dreams, they intertwine.

Through fields of green, they softly drift,
Offering hope, a precious gift.
In every rustle, truths are found,
Beneath the sky, above the ground.

Chasing shadows, they weave and twine,
Invisible threads, a grand design.
With every sigh, they long to share,
The hidden tales that float in air.

As twilight falls, the night sets in,
The secrets swirl, new journeys begin.
In the moonlight's glow, whispers remain,
In the dance of the night, they sing again.

Echoes of the Tempest

Thundering skies, the storm awakens,
In shadows deep, the earth is shaken.
Lightning strikes, a brilliant flash,
Nature's roar, a wild clash.

Raindrops fall like fleeting tears,
Washing away the hidden fears.
In every beat, a heartbeat thunders,
Echoes of life, in nature's wonders.

Winds howl fierce, they dance with rage,
Turning the world, a tempest stage.
Each gust sings of power untamed,
In the storm's heart, wildness named.

But after the storm, the calm will rise,
With gentle winds and clear blue skies.
From chaos to peace, the cycle flows,
In every tempest, life still grows.

Chasing the Zephyr

A soft caress, the zephyr calls,
With every breath, the spirit enthralls.
Across the fields, where daisies lie,
It dances low, beneath the sky.

Whispers of spring in every sway,
A fleeting touch, come out to play.
With wings of air, it skips with grace,
Inviting all to join the chase.

Rustling leaves, it weaves its tale,
A gentle guide on a winding trail.
Through valleys deep and mountains wide,
With open hearts, we roam beside.

As day departs and stars ignite,
The zephyr carries the warmth of light.
In evening's hush, we breathe anew,
Forever chasing the sky's bright blue.

Anemone's Embrace

In the garden where colors bloom,
Anemones sway, dispelling gloom.
Petals stretch in the morning light,
Embraced by warmth, a beautiful sight.

Whispers of spring in a gentle dance,
Nature's canvas, a fleeting chance.
Each soft wave holds a secret sweet,
In every fold, where shadows meet.

Among the flowers, bees hum and play,
As dusk approaches, they find their way.
The moon bids farewell to the sunny race,
In the twilight, there's anemone's grace.

Gentle Ribbons of Air

Breezes weave through the willow leaves,
Whispers of stories the forest retrieves.
Dancing lightly, they twirl and bow,
Painting the skies, enchanting now.

Carried along, where the wildflowers grow,
Caressing the petals, a soft, sweet flow.
Gentle ribbons of air, they glide,
In the heart of nature, they love to hide.

With every sigh, they connect and link,
Vibrant and lively, they beckon to think.
Of moments fleeting, of laughter shared,
In the embrace of wind, we are ensnared.

Echoes in the Stillness

In the silence, where shadows creep,
Echoes linger, secrets to keep.
Footsteps fade on the ancient ground,
Their stories whispered, never found.

Stillness speaks in a hushed refrain,
Time stands still like lingering rain.
Below the surface, echoes persist,
A gentle reminder of what we miss.

In the twilight, moments entwine,
Fleeting wisps of a world divine.
Though silence reigns and night draws nigh,
Echoes linger, never to die.

The Dancer's Embrace

Beneath the lights, in a world so bright,
The dancer spins, lost in delight.
Graceful movements through the air,
Capturing hearts with each flair.

Every turn tells a story sweet,
In rhythmic beats, she finds her beat.
An embrace of art and soul,
In every leap, she feels whole.

The music swells, and the night unfolds,
Through laughter and dreams, her spirit bold.
In the moment, she twirls with grace,
In the dancer's embrace, time leaves no trace.

Kaleidoscope in Flight

Colors dance in the sky,
A tapestry made of dreams,
Wings spread wide to fly,
Life bursting at the seams.

Twists and turns of the breeze,
A canvas bright and swirling,
Nature's art is sure to please,
In spirals, joy unfurling.

With every shade, a new delight,
Moments captured, swift and fleeting,
The heart takes wing, feels light,
In the harmony of greeting.

Dance on, wonder in sight,
In a world of endless motion,
Kaleidoscope, pure and bright,
Soars on waves of sweet emotion.

Serenade of the Whispering Pines

Beneath the trees, soft sighs flow,
Nature hums a gentle tune,
In the twilight's golden glow,
Stars awaken, silver moon.

Leaves converse in mystic tones,
Echoes of the past arise,
Timber whispers, ancient groans,
Cradled under open skies.

Every rustle, a sweet prayer,
Voices bond, entwined as one,
Softly drifting through the air,
Harmony 'til day is done.

In this realm of peace and grace,
The heart finds solace, deep and true,
Embraced by nature's warm embrace,
The serenade will carry you.

Tempestuous Lullabies

Storm clouds gather, shadows cling,
Whispers ride on thunder's back,
Dance of chaos, turmoil's fling,
Nature's symphony, off the track.

Yet in the tempest's fierce embrace,
A lullaby begins to weave,
Softening the winds that race,
Cradling hearts that long to believe.

Raindrops fall like soothing tears,
Melodies that cleanse the night,
In the chaos, calm draws near,
Inviting peace by sheer delight.

Tempests roar, but softly sigh,
In the eye, the world stands still,
From stormy echoes, a gentle cry,
Find tranquility, if you will.

Whirlwinds of Emotion

Feelings twirl in dizzying dance,
Storms of joy, waves of despair,
Each moment holds a fleeting chance,
To savor life's breath of air.

Hearts like leaves in autumn whirl,
Caught in the tempest's playful chase,
Dreams and doubts in circles twirl,
In this wild, chaotic space.

Crimson skies and twilight blue,
Every hue a story told,
Emotions merge, a vibrant brew,
In the whirlwind, hearts grow bold.

Ride the currents, take the leap,
Let passion guide and lead you on,
In life's whirlwinds, secrets keep,
With each turn, a new dawn.

Flowing through Time

Moments slip like grains of sand,
Memories etched by gentle hands.
Time flows softly, a river wide,
Carrying dreams on its steady tide.

Whispers of ages, secrets old,
Stories shared and tales foretold.
Each heartbeat marks the passage true,
As we journey on, just me and you.

Past and future, a dance so bright,
Guided by stars in the velvet night.
Each blink a story, each sigh a rhyme,
We are the echoes, flowing through time.

Under the Canopy of Sky

Beneath the vast and azure dome,
We find our hearts, we feel at home.
Clouds drift gently, soft as lace,
In nature's arms, we find our place.

The sun's warm glow, a golden thread,
Weave through dreams, where souls are fed.
Birds sing sweetly, a joyful choir,
In the open sky, our spirits soar higher.

The evening's hues, a deep embrace,
Stars unveil in the endless space.
Together we stand, hand in hand,
Under the canopy, so grand.

Whispers of wind, tales untold,
Nature's wonders, a sight to behold.
In twilight's hold, we feel alive,
Under the sky, our dreams will thrive.

Beneath the Sails of Dream

Waves of wonder crash and play,
In the realm where night meets day.
Beneath the sails, our hopes are cast,
Into the sea of dreams, so vast.

Stars above like jewels gleam,
Guiding our hearts, igniting the dream.
The wind's soft sigh, a tender plea,
As we navigate the deep blue sea.

Each horizon whispers of chance,
Pulling us into the timeless dance.
With every breeze, our spirits rise,
Beneath the sails, we touch the skies.

We chart our course through depths unknown,
In this magical world, we have grown.
Together we'll sail, forever free,
Beneath the sails of our wildest dream.

Driftwood Dreams

Washed ashore by the salty tide,
Driftwood rests where secrets hide.
Smooth and worn by ocean's grace,
Each piece holds time's gentle trace.

Stories linger in the wood's grain,
Echoes of journeys, joy, and pain.
In twilight's glow, we gather near,
Sharing tales of love and fear.

Twisted forms, a rustic charm,
In humble beauty, they disarm.
We carve our dreams on every piece,
In driftwood's arms, we find our peace.

Together we build, with nature's art,
A sanctuary for the soul and heart.
In every wave, a memory streams,
Among the driftwood, we weave our dreams.

Gentle Murmurs Over Mountains

Whispers flow through canyon's veil,
Where echoes of the past set sail.
Each breeze brings tales, soft and low,
In twilight's grip, the soft winds blow.

Beneath the stars, the world feels small,
Nature beckons, a gentle call.
With every step on rugged stone,
The mountain's heart beats all alone.

Hidden paths where wildflowers grow,
Tread softly where the rivers flow.
In quiet strength, the mountains rise,
Guarding secrets 'neath the skies.

As dawn arrives, the shadows fade,
A canvas bright, the night has made.
With gentle murmurs, they remind,
Of tranquil thoughts in nature's kind.

The Journey of an Untamed Whirlwind

A tempest born from restless dreams,
It dances wild through scattered beams.
With every twist, a new verse played,
The world below, in motion swayed.

Through fields of gold and forests deep,
The untamed whirlwind does not sleep.
It gathers strength, a force of might,
Chasing echoes into the night.

Over mountains, it races fast,
A fleeting glimpse, then gone at last.
It stirs the leaves and bends the trees,
An artist free, unbound by ease.

As sunlight fades, the shadows creep,
This journey wild, a secret keep.
With every laugh, the storm does sing,
A melody, a wild, free thing.

Dreams Whispered Through the Trees

In the quiet of the night,
Dreams take wing beyond the light.
Through the branches, soft and clear,
Whispers call, inviting near.

Tales of wonder, moonlit skies,
Emerge like stars in children's eyes.
Beneath the boughs, where spirits play,
The heart finds peace, the mind may stray.

With gentle winds, the secrets flow,
From cedar roots to rivers low.
In every rustle, hope entwines,
A world of dreams, where love defines.

In twilight's hush, we close our eyes,
And let the dreams soar through the skies.
Where trees embrace, the truth reveals,
The magic that each moment steals.

Shadows Cast by High Altitudes

On mountain peaks where eagles cry,
Shadows stretch beneath the sky.
Nature's hand, so grand, so bold,
Tells stories of the brave and old.

With every breeze, the whispers flow,
In shadows deep, the secrets grow.
The heights may lift, but shadows fall,
A dance of light that grips us all.

Among the stones, the silence speaks,
In every crack, the history leaks.
Where grounded roots meet endless blue,
The world reflects a different view.

As sunset glows and day turns dim,
The shadows dance on every whim.
In high altitudes, we find our place,
Beneath the stars, the moon's embrace.

The Art of Air's Embrace

In twilight's glow, the currents tease,
A dance of whispers through the trees.
Each breath a brushstroke on the sky,
A fleeting moment, sweet and shy.

The wings of dreams upon the rise,
Carried forth by breath's soft sighs.
In silence, stories intertwine,
The art of air, so pure, divine.

With every gust, the secrets flow,
An artist's hand in nature's show.
A tapestry of soft caress,
The heart finds peace in air's finesse.

In the gentle touch, we find our way,
In the art of air, we wish to stay.
A world of wonder, vast and bright,
Embraced by whispers of the night.

Unfurling Horizons of Time

In twilight's embrace, the past unfurls,
  Stories linger, like over spun pearls.
Every moment, a thread we weave,
  In the fabric of time, we believe.

Horizons stretch, where dreams reside,
  Past and future in tender stride.
Each heartbeat holds a new design,
  In the unfurling, love will shine.

Echoes of laughter, shadows of pain,
  Memories dance in the gentle rain.
Time's tapestry, rich, sublime,
  Unfurling softly, like warm sunshine.

Together we journey through the night,
  Woven in whispers, pure delight.
With every dawn, futures ignite,
  Unfurling horizons, taking flight.

Whispers in the Breeze

The breeze carries secrets, light and free,
Melodies of nature's symphony.
In every rustle, a story told,
Whispers of silver, whispers of gold.

Through fields of grass, the murmurs glide,
Echoes of love where shadows hide.
In gentle currents, hearts can soar,
Whispers in the breeze, forevermore.

Each leaf a letter, a page unfurled,
Messages shared from a distant world.
With every sigh, the spirits tease,
Life is a song that flows with ease.

Embrace the whispers, soft and sweet,
In nature's arms, our worlds shall meet.
Together we dance with time's own breeze,
Finding our peace in gentle seas.

Breath of the Earth

From mountain peaks to valleys deep,
The earth exhales, its secrets keep.
In every stone, a tale lies bare,
The breath of the earth, light as air.

Rivers hum a timeless tune,
Beneath the sun and watchful moon.
In sighs of winds, a lullaby,
The earth speaks softly, time goes by.

Roots entwined in ancient ground,
In whispered echoes, wisdom found.
Nature's pulse, a steady beat,
The breath of the earth, rich and sweet.

With open hearts, we heed the call,
Together, we rise, together, we fall.
In every heartbeat, in every mirth,
We share the breath, the breath of earth.

Secrets of the Whispering Woods

In the shadows where tall trees sway,
A gentle breeze begins to play.
Soft murmurs rise from the forest floor,
Tales of old echo, forevermore.

Hidden paths lead to secrets deep,
Where quiet creatures softly creep.
Rustling leaves like whispers shared,
In the woods, a voice that's bared.

Moonlight dances on silver streams,
Carrying hopes and fading dreams.
Ancient roots with stories woven,
In every shade, a truth unspoken.

Every step upon the ground,
In this sanctuary, solace found.
Listen closely, hear the call,
In the woods, we are one and all.

A Drift Across the Meadow

Beneath the sky, a canvas wide,
Where wildflowers dance and glide.
Soft petals sway in the gentle air,
In the meadow, joy is rare.

A drift of color, bright and bold,
Tales of seasons yet untold.
Butterflies flit with graceful ease,
Whispers echo with the breeze.

Sunlight spills on emerald blades,
Golden hour in tranquil shades.
Nature's quilt, a patchwork view,
In this haven, life feels new.

Moments captured, forever seen,
In a blissful, vibrant green.
Wander here, let worries go,
In the meadow, hearts will glow.

Gales of Reflection

Upon the cliffs, where seagulls cry,
The winds carry whispers high.
Memories drift like clouds in flight,
In the gales, both day and night.

With each gust, the past returns,
Lessons learned, and wisdom earns.
The waves crash against the stone,
In their roar, the heart finds home.

Moonlit tides recede and flow,
In their rhythm, peace we know.
Nature sings a somber tune,
Underneath the silver moon.

In stillness found between the blasts,
A moment cherished, never past.
The gales remind us of our quest,
In reflection, we find our rest.

Where the Breezes Meet

At the horizon's edge, they twine,
Warm and cool, a dance divine.
Gentle whispers brush the skin,
In this place, the day begins.

Rivers wind where soft winds drift,
Nature's heart, a sacred gift.
Here, the laughter of leaves sways,
As sunlight blends with twilight's rays.

Clouds embrace in tender grace,
Painting skies in a warm embrace.
In the silence, dreams take flight,
Where breezes meet, hearts ignite.

Boundless skies, a hopeful spree,
In this realm, we are set free.
Feel the magic, let it bloom,
Where breezes meet, find your room.

Lightness of Being

In the dawn's gentle glow, reach high,
Where dreams dance softly, like a sigh.
Moments drift on whispers of air,
Carrying laughter, light without care.

Hearts beat in rhythm, a joyous song,
In the flow of life, where we belong.
With every step, let burdens fade,
Embrace the grace in the choices made.

The Embrace of Nature

Beneath the boughs, where shadows play,
The rustle of leaves invites the day.
With every breath, the earth inspires,
Whispers of hope in the gentle fires.

Mountains rise, steadfast and grand,
Holding secrets in the silent land.
Streams dance lightly over stones so old,
Tales of the ages in their waters told.

A Sky Full of Stories

Above us stretch the endless skies,
Where each cloud carries tales that rise.
Stars wink softly, secrets they keep,
In the night, where dreams are deep.

Colors bloom at the break of dawn,
Painting the world in hues reborn.
Each sunset whispers, a fleeting glance,
Time slows down in nature's dance.

The Essence of Exploration

With each new path, the spirit soars,
Inviting hearts to wander, to explore.
Mountains, rivers, each twist and turn,
In the quest for knowledge, we yearn.

Beneath the stars, we find our way,
In the thrill of night, a bright array.
Every journey leaves a mark,
In the soul's compass, igniting sparks.

The Abyss of Air

In whispers deep where shadows dwell,
The silence hums a ghostly spell.
Beneath the veil of endless night,
The stars are lost, a fading light.

A breath away from dreams untold,
The winds of fate begin to fold.
A dance of thoughts, a fleeting glance,
In twilight's grip, we chance a dance.

The echoes rise, as fears take flight,
In depths unseen, we seek the light.
A journey starts with every sigh,
In the abyss, the spirits fly.

Embrace the void, the vast unknown,
For in this space, our seeds are sown.
In every breath, a world to share,
Together, we find solace there.

A Fable in Flight

Once told in dreams, a tale takes wing,
Of creatures bold and the songs they sing.
In skies of azure, they roam so free,
Their laughter dances like leaves on a tree.

A little bird with feathers bright,
Chased the sun through day to night.
It whispered secrets in the breeze,
Of love and loss among the trees.

A wise old owl, with eyes like fire,
Spoke of wisdom, and truths to inspire.
With tales of old and paths once tread,
They wove a fable, a thread well-spread.

In gentle winds, their stories soar,
A bond unbroken, forever more.
In every heart, these legends stay,
A fable in flight, come what may.

Roaming in the Clear Blue

Beneath the sky so vast and bright,
We wander forth in pure delight.
The sea of dreams stretches ahead,
With every step, new paths to tread.

Mountains rise like ancient guards,
In fields of gold, we cast our cards.
The whispers of the wind invite,
A journey glowing in the light.

Clouds drift softly, painted hues,
We chase the shadows, dance in blues.
Each moment fleeting, yet profound,
In open air, our hearts are found.

With every breath, the world expands,
In the clear blue, we make our stands.
United in this grand pursuit,
We find our voices, brave and astute.

Fluttering Secrets

In gardens lush, where whispers flow,
Fluttering secrets in sunlight glow.
Petals dance on a morning breeze,
Each one holds tales, meant to please.

A butterfly flits with grace divine,
Bringing stories along the vine.
It knows the songs of days gone by,
In every flutter, a silent sigh.

Hidden laughter under leaves so green,
In nature's arms, life feels serene.
The mute parade of colors bright,
In silence, they reveal their light.

With every flutter, a truth unfolds,
Secrets of life, in silence told.
Embrace the quiet, hear them sing,
For in each heart, we find our wing.

The Dance of Leaves in Twilight

Whispers of breeze in the fading light,
Leaves twirl and spin in a graceful flight.
Shadows stretch long as the day fades away,
Nature's soft symphony bids night to stay.

Glistening amber, the branches sway,
In hues of gold, as the sun drifts away.
A rustling chorus sings sweet to the moon,
Echoing softly, embracing the tune.

Under a canopy bathed in dusk,
Each leaf's soft dance is a delicate musk.
Moments unravel like silk in the air,
Nature's own rhythm, serene and rare.

In twilight's embrace, hearts intertwine,
As the trees weave their tales into vine.
With every breath, life's wonders are spun,
The dance of the leaves, a magic begun.

Riddles Carried from Distant Shores

Whispers of waves hold secrets untold,
Stories of sailors, adventures bold.
Crumbling maps where the legends reside,
Riddles of oceans swirling like tide.

Forgotten treasures in sand's gentle grip,
Echoes of voyages on a long-lost ship.
Mysteries linger on the breeze's breath,
Life's fleeting moments, entwined with death.

Shells speak of journeys on vibrant seas,
Chasing the horizon with fervent ease.
Footprints washed away by the limitless foam,
Whispers of wanderers searching for home.

From the depths of history, stories arise,
Tales of the brave and the valiant skies.
Riddles carried forth with the winds' soft sigh,
Forever entwined with the world's lullaby.

Secrets of the Horizon's Edge

Where the sky kisses the endless sea,
Secrets lie deep in tranquility.
Waves that dance under twilight's embrace,
Guard the whispers of time and space.

Clouds paint the canvas with strokes of gold,
Stories unfold that are ages old.
Beyond the horizon, dreams take their flight,
A place where the dark blooms into the light.

Voyagers linger at the brink of the day,
Searching for meaning as shadows play.
The horizon beckons with a silent call,
In the breath of the dusk, we rise and fall.

On the edge of the world, where hopes are spun,
Every sunset tells of battles won.
In the twilight's glow, let your spirit roam,
Secrets of the horizon lead us back home.

The Flight Path of Celestial Sighs

Stars shimmering softly, a celestial map,
Guiding our dreams through a velvet gap.
From the heavens, whispers of love take wing,
In the still of the night, where memories cling.

Eclipsed in shadows, the moonlight shall dance,
Casting a spell in a mystical trance.
Each twinkle a story, a prayer to the skies,
The flight path unfolds through the softest sighs.

Galaxies twirling in a waltz so bright,
Leading us onward, through the velvet night.
In the tapestry woven by time's gentle hand,
Celestial secrets on stardust we stand.

So let your heart soar with the wings of a dream,
Touched by the light of a cosmic beam.
The flight path of whispers and hopes set high,
In the expanse of eternity, watch us fly.

Carrion of the Silent Zephyr

In dusk's embrace, shadows creep,
The air hangs thick, secrets to keep.
Fallen whispers, time unbends,
A quiet sigh, where silence ends.

Beneath the stars, remnants lie,
Forgotten dreams, a lingering sigh.
Nature mourns what once was bright,
In the stillness, fades the light.

Skyward Wishes

Wishes take flight on feathered wings,
Carried high by gentle springs.
In a world where dreams ignite,
Hope ascends, embracing light.

Each breath a story, untold and free,
Mountains whisper of what could be.
As the clouds dance with the sun,
Skyward wishes, hearts as one.

The Language of Air

Whispers travel on a breeze,
Secrets woven through the trees.
In every gust, a tale is spun,
Silent voices, softly run.

Gentle sighs beneath the moon,
Lullabies that speak too soon.
In the still, a message shared,
The language of air, souls declared.

Motion in the Stillness

Amidst the calm, a pulse resides,
The heart beats where silence hides.
Ripples form in quiet streams,
Life awakens, the world dreams.

Leaves tremble with a subtle touch,
Nature whispers, soft as such.
In stillness found, a dance unfolds,
Motion breathes where time beholds.

Spirit of Flutter

In the quiet morn, wings take flight,
Dancing on whispers, light and bright.
Colors collide in the softest breeze,
Nature's soft chorus, the heart feels ease.

Through the sun's warm rays, soft shadows fall,
Graceful arcs twirl, a celestial call.
In the gentle sway of the fragrant flowers,
Time slips away, lost in the hours.

A flutter of wings, a moment's delight,
The spirit takes wing, out of sight.
A fleeting dance, one with the sky,
A reminder of dreams that never die.

Whispers of peace in the air around,
In every flutter, a joy is found.
Infinite dreams as soft as a sigh,
In the spirit of flutter, we learn to fly.

Wings of Serenity

Beneath the vastness, the calm unfolds,
Wings stretched wide, stories untold.
Gentle breezes cradle the soul,
In the dance of the skies, we become whole.

Clouds embrace the day's soft glow,
In their shadows, the world moves slow.
Peace lingers where the heart takes flight,
In the tranquility of the fading light.

Gliding through whispers, the stillness sings,
Life in the balance on delicate wings.
Every breath a promise, softly shared,
In the grace of the moment, deeply cared.

A journey of stillness, the heart finds rest,
In the wings of serenity, we are blessed.
Floating on dreams, in silence we thrive,
Embracing the calm, we learn to be alive.

A Journey on the Breath

Inhale the whispers of morning's light,
Exhale the shadows that fade from sight.
With every breath, a story unfolds,
A journey within, where truth beholds.

Feel the pulse of the earth beneath,
Rhythms of life, in silence, we breathe.
Each moment a canvas, pure and clear,
In the heart's gentle whispers, we draw near.

Time flows like streams in the open air,
Carrying dreams, our burden laid bare.
Through valleys of stillness, we wander free,
In the journey on breath, we find our key.

As the sun dips low and night prevails,
We trace our steps through celestial trails.
Every sigh a reminder, a sacred thread,
In the journey on breath, we move ahead.

Shimmering Airborne Threads

In the twilight's glow, the tendrils dance,
Shimmering brightly, caught in a glance.
Threads of silver weave through the skies,
A tapestry of dreams that gently flies.

Every flutter glimmers, a sparkling show,
In the heart of the night, the whispers grow.
With starlit paths on an endless thread,
We journey onward where angels tread.

Cascading colors in the evening air,
Embracing the magic that lingers there.
In the shadows, the promise unfurls,
A symphony sweet, spun from the pearls.

Through the shimmering threads, our spirits soar,
In the night's embrace, we search for more.
With each delicate weave, we unite in grace,
In the shimmering airborne, we find our place.

Celestial Conversations

Stars whisper secrets in the night,
Drifting on waves of silver light.
Planets spin in graceful dance,
Creating dreams with every glance.

Galaxies twirl in cosmic play,
Lighting paths in a grand display.
Comets streak with tails aglow,
Leaving traces of tales untold.

Nebulas bloom in colors bright,
Stitching the fabric of endless night.
Asteroids wander, lonely and old,
Sharing mysteries that they hold.

In this vast universe we exist,
Every moment a cosmic twist.
As whispers rise in the dark expanse,
We find meaning in the stars' romance.

The Singing Winds

Winds carry songs from far away,
Lifting voices as they sway.
Through the trees their stories flow,
In melodies soft, they ebb and glow.

Gentle breezes brush our skin,
Awakening the life within.
Rustling leaves in rhythmic tune,
Dancing softly under the moon.

Whispers echo on mountain tops,
In valleys deep, the silence stops.
Every gust a tale to share,
Of distant lands and dreams laid bare.

With every breath, the world evolves,
In the wind's embrace, life resolves.
A symphony of nature's grace,
Reminds us of our shared space.

Dancing Through the Night

Underneath a tapestry of stars,
We twirl as if no one knows who we are.
Moonlight bathes us in silver sheen,
In this moment, we're free and keen.

Footsteps echo on soft cool grass,
As shadows blend and flicker, they pass.
Hearts align with the rhythm of time,
In the air, a sweet, haunting chime.

Whirl and spin, let spirits soar,
In the glow, we lose evermore.
Hands entwined, a gentle hold,
In the stillness, stories unfold.

As night deepens, our laughter sings,
The world falls away, and freedom springs.
Together we dance through dreams in flight,
Forever lost, in the heart of the night.

Shifting Skylines

Cities rise like dreams on high,
Reaching fingers toward the sky.
Skylines shift, a constant change,
As life unfolds in every range.

Glass and steel like rivers gleam,
Reflecting wishes, hopes, and dreams.
Each building tells a tale anew,
Of lives well-lived and journeys true.

In the sunset's glow, they stand proud,
Bold silhouettes against the cloud.
In dawn's embrace, they breathe and sigh,
Witnessing moments that pass by.

Through seasons' dance, they bend and sway,
Echoing stories of yesterday.
In every shift, a chance to see,
The beauty of change, forever free.